FAITHFUL
STEWARDS

THE WORD UNLEASHED

A Ministry of Countryside Bible Church

Southlake, TX

FAITHFUL
STEWARDS

TOM PENNINGTON

Unless otherwise indicated, all Scripture quotations are taken from the New American Standard Bible ®, © 1960, 1962, 1963, 1968, 1971, 1972, 1973, 1975, 1977, 1995 by the Lockman Foundation. Used by permission. (www.Lockman.org)

Cover by Alister MacInnes

Faithful Stewards
© 2022 by Tom Pennington

Published by © The Word Unleashed
www.thewordunleashed.org
PO Box 96077
Southlake, TX 76092

The Word Unleashed is a ministry of Countryside Bible Church in Southlake, TX.
www.countrysidebible.org

ISBN - 979-8-9857172-2-8

All rights reserved. No part of this book may be reproduced, or transmitted in any form or by any means—electronic, mechanical, digital, photocopy, recording, or any other—except for brief quotations in printed reviews, without the prior permission of the publisher.

Printed in the United States of America.

To John MacArthur who has been a faithful steward for over 50 years, and whose life and ministry have indelibly marked my own.

SERIES PREFACE

The *Faithful Stewards* series exists to encourage pastors and leaders of local churches as they pursue faithful, biblical ministry. In 1 Corinthians 4, the apostle Paul reminds us that God will not measure our ministries by their results—whether outward success or failure. We contribute nothing to the spiritual results of our efforts. Only God can give life to dead hearts through the gospel—regeneration (Jas. 1:18). And only His Spirit can transform the hearts of His people through His Word—sanctification (John 17:17; 2 Cor. 3:18). All that God requires of us is to be *faithful stewards*. Paul writes, "This is how one should regard us, as servants of Christ and stewards of the mysteries of God. Moreover, it is required of stewards that they be found faithful" (1 Cor. 4:1–2 ESV).

Our chief assignment as stewards is to be faithful with the "mysteries of God" revealed in the Word of God. Church leaders have many responsibilities in Christ's church, but our chief duty, our primary task, is to *feed* His sheep! We must first be faithful stewards of the Word of God and the gospel of our Lord Jesus Christ.

Remember who holds the final verdict on our ministries. It is not the unbelieving world around us or the churches we serve. Not even our own personal assessment really matters. Only Christ's final verdict matters.

When we stand before His Judgment Seat, He will base His assessment primarily on whether we have handled "accurately the word of truth" (2 Tim. 2:15). He even measures our love for Him on how faithfully we feed the sheep He loves and died for (John 21:15–17). May God help us to make the primary aim of our ministries to be *faithful stewards*.

"Let a man regard us in this manner, as servants of Christ and stewards of the mysteries of God. In this case, moreover, it is required of stewards that one be found trustworthy. But to me it is a very small thing that I may be examined by you, or by any human court; in fact, I do not even examine myself. For I am conscious of nothing against myself, yet I am not by this acquitted; but the one who examines me is the Lord. Therefore do not go on passing judgment before the time, but wait until the Lord comes who will both bring to light the things hidden in the darkness and disclose the motives of men's hearts; and then each man's praise will come to him from God."

1 CORINTHIANS 4:1-5

FAITHFUL STEWARDS

During a famous scene in William Shakespeare's play *Henry V*, Henry Plantagenet makes an impassioned speech to his outnumbered and beleaguered troops as they prepare for battle in the Hundred Years' War. He says, "We few, we happy few, we band of brothers; for he today, who sheds his blood with me will be my brother."[1]

Plantagenet's words capture the heart of serving in pastoral ministry: pastors and church leaders are in a war on behalf of our great General, the Lord Jesus Christ. In our time, men who are willing to fight in this war are few. But those who have been saved by Christ and are

---

1   *Henry V*, Act 4, Scene 3.

willing to courageously fight for Him are truly a band of brothers in a lifelong battle for our Lord and His gospel.

As you assess your ministry—your corner of the battlefield—how would you describe your relationships with the leaders and members of your church? Are they healthy relationships of mutual respect and honor that is evident to all?

Some pastors are admired to an unhealthy degree—church members practically worship the ground they walk on. Others serve in difficult situations in which their genuine love and affection for their people is seldom reciprocated and members don't appear to respect or honor their leaders at all. Many disapprove of their ministry, respond slowly to the teaching of Scripture, and even blame the pastor for problems in the church.

Being a leader in our Lord's church is hazardous duty. Though there are mountaintop experiences that cause our spirits to soar into the presence of God Himself, there are also dark valleys of discouragement and loneliness. Sometimes, we traverse the highest heights and the deepest lows on the same day.

Moses experienced both the highs and lows of ministry in one day's time when he enjoyed communion with the pre-incarnate Christ on Mount Sinai (Exod. 19–31) and then immediately dealt with the gross immorality of the golden calf incident in Exodus 32. Elijah saw God rain down fire on Mount Carmel, yet within twenty-four hours he was running to the desert in fear for his life (1 Kings 18–19).

Even our Lord experienced very similar situations. Mark 3:20–27 records multitudes gathered around Jesus to hear Him teach, as His unbelieving brothers arrived to take him by force back to Nazareth because they thought He was out of his mind! At the same time, the Pharisees accused Him of being in league with the devil.

You have probably experienced similar days in your ministry. As pastors in Christ's church, how are we to respond to these situations?

How are we to maintain spiritual stability in light of the various responses we receive? What is the key to maintaining our spiritual equilibrium in pastoral ministry? The answer is found in the apostle Paul's first letter to the Corinthians.

THE APOSTOLIC MODEL

The leaders and members of the church in Corinth had widely differing perspectives toward Paul and his ministry. Some undoubtedly had a balanced, biblical view of him and his leadership. Some elevated him inordinately (1 Cor. 3:4). Others practically demonized him: they said his personality was weak and unimpressive, his message was simplistic and lacked true, profound wisdom, and the style of his preaching was missing the rhetorical polish they expected from their speakers (1 Cor. 2:1–5). They also questioned his motives. In fact, some even speculated that he was in ministry for money and sexual favors from women (1 Cor. 9:1–18). This group treated Paul as the scapegoat for everything that was wrong in the Corinthian church.

Regardless, by God's grace, Paul faithfully served alongside the Corinthians for 18 months. Even after he departed, he continued to shepherd them from afar.

Amid hero worship from some and contempt from others, how was Paul able to stay the course? How did he keep his ministerial balance as people responded to him in a variety of ways? How was he able to preserve the quality and effectiveness of his ministry?

In 1 Corinthians 4, under the inspiration of the Holy Spirit, Paul records a biblical mindset for surviving the trials and triumphs of ministry. He provides a healthy model for responding to the highs and lows of ministry. This mindset should characterize the ministry of every faithful pastor and church leader.

Paul's example will keep us from believing and falling prey to our fan club (and we all have a fan club of some kind). We must guard against believing them to avoid having exalted views of ourselves. The apostle's example will also keep us from being discouraged and beaten down by detractors. Paul's actions not only provide a wonderful example of how we should *think* about leadership in Christ's church, but they reveal how we should *respond* in the highs and lows of ministry. In 1 Corinthians 4:1–5 he writes,

> Let a man regard us in this manner as servants of Christ and stewards of the mysteries of God. In this case, moreover, it is required of stewards that one be found trustworthy. But to me it is a very small thing that I may be examined by you or by any human court. In fact, I do not even examine myself. For I am conscious of nothing against myself, yet I am not by this acquitted. But the one who examines me is the Lord. Therefore, do not go on passing judgment before the time, but wait until the Lord comes, who will both bring to light the things hidden

in the darkness and disclose the motives of men's hearts. And then each man's praise will come to him from God.

Out of the many serious problems wreaking havoc in the Corinthian church, one in particular stood out to Paul. Different groups within the church had associated themselves with well-known Christian leaders. A series of quarrels and divisions broke out and a partisan spirit infected the entire church. Paul writes, "I have been informed concerning you, my brethren, by Chloe's *people*, that there are quarrels among you. Now I mean this, that each one of you is saying, 'I am of Paul,' and 'I of Apollos,' and 'I of Cephas,' and 'I of Christ'" (1 Cor. 1:11–12). Paul recognized that the real problem fueling the division inside the church was a misconception of the nature of Christian leadership.

Beginning in 1 Corinthians 3, Paul corrects the divisiveness, teaching all the Corinthians to think rightly about the nature of spiritual leadership. This is the same pattern that subsequent generations of Christian leaders must follow.

In 1 Corinthians 4:1–5, Paul prescribes three key perspectives on church leadership that will help us maintain our spiritual stability through the highs and lows of ministry. These perspectives enable us to see through the accolades and criticisms that invariably come with ministry.

REMEMBER OUR REAL POSITION

The first perspective about church leadership Paul models and explains is that we must remember our real position. The fleshly attitudes of some of the Corinthians had caused them to exalt their leaders. Unfortunately, some of the leaders tolerated this behavior and probably even encouraged it. Paul sets out to explain the attitude that all the Corinthians, including its leaders, should have toward leadership in the church. He writes, "What then is Apollos? And what is Paul? Servants through whom you believed even as the Lord gave *opportunity* to each one" (1 Cor. 3:5).

In presenting his case, Paul uses three powerful metaphors to illustrate the mindset that must be cultivated in church leadership (1

Cor. 3:5–4:1). First, he employs an agricultural metaphor. He refers to all believers as God's field (3:5–9), and the leaders of the church, including Paul, Peter, and Apollos, as workers in God's field.

Second, Paul uses an architectural metaphor. He compares the church to a temple that's being built: the church is God's building, and its leaders are construction workers in the massive building project (3:9–17).

Paul then introduces a third metaphor: leaders are servants, serving Christ in a great household. Paul writes, "Let a man regard us in this manner as servants of Christ and stewards of the mysteries of God" (4:1). The imperative "regard" is the normal New Testament word for *reckon*, which means to establish value based on careful calculation. Paul commands the Corinthians to calculate the value of the church's leaders in this way. This was exactly how Paul thought of his own leadership. It's the mindset the Corinthians should have had of its leaders, and it's the mindset our church members must have. As shepherds of

God's flock, this is how we must think about our leadership in the church where God has placed us.

The word translated "servants" occurs only here in the New Testament. In classical Greek, it referred to the bottom level of rowers on a galley. By the first century, *servants* lost that specific meaning and came to mean anyone who served as an assistant or received orders from another person.[2]

God's Word tells us to think of ourselves as servants and assistants of Christ—we directly report to, and take orders from, Him. Our ministry position is that of humble assistants of our Lord and Savior. We're never to think of our position as an exalted one. We are not, and will never be, the head of the Church (Eph. 5:18; Col. 1:18). We are not its CEO, and we must never think of, or promote ourselves, as such. Rather, when we

---

2   *Servants* (ὑπηρέτης) is most often used in the New Testament to describe the junior officers in the Temple Guard (Matt. 26:58; Mark 14:54, 65). It's also used to identify the attendant who put away the Isaiah scroll that Jesus read publicly (Luke 4:20). In the book of Acts, it describes John Mark, who assisted Paul and Barnabas on their first missionary journey (Acts 13:5).

contemplate our position in Christ's church, we must remember that we are not just leaders, but *servant* leaders.

In Mark 10:43–44, our Lord made it very clear what kind of leadership was to characterize His kingdom: "Whoever wishes to become great among you shall be your servant; and whoever wishes to be first among you shall be slave of all." Jesus' words remind us of our rightful position as assistants of Christ. Our only significance in ministry is that we have a relationship with Him. David Garland writes, "Ministers work under the orders of their master and have no significance except in relation to their master."[3]

Ultimately, the church is not our responsibility because the field is not ours; we're merely laborers in it. The building is not ours; we're just workers in it. Even the household is not ours; we're merely servants in it. That's our real position in ministry, and we must fully embrace it.

---

3 David Garland, *1 Corinthians*, Baker Exegetical Commentary on the New Testament (Grand Rapids: Baker, 2003), 125.

Faithful Stewards

There's one specific category of servants Paul highlights: stewards. First Corinthians 4:1 says we're "*stewards* of the mysteries of God" (emphasis added). Not only are we assistants of Christ, but as our Master and Lord, He has assigned us the specific duty of being His stewards.

In the first century, stewards were servants who managed the day-to-day affairs of a great house or large estate. He was assigned to oversee the remainder of the household, including his master's possessions (Luke 16:1, 3). From those goods, the steward gave the rest of the servants their daily rations (Luke 12:42). Galatians 4:1–2 says that stewards even supervised the children of their masters until they came of age.

As pastors, we're also called to be stewards. We oversee God's household in the local churches we serve (Titus 1:7). The church is not our house, and we don't get to establish our own plans for ministry—God does! We have no right to make independent decisions about God's household. Instead, we must handle His directives with care and willingly submit to how He wants His household to run. John Calvin writes,

> "[Pastors] ought to apply themselves not to their work but that of the Lord, who has hired them as his servants, and that they are not appointed to bear rule in an authoritative manner in the church, but are subject to Christ's authority—in short, that they are servants, not masters."[4]

Charles Hodge adds, "Ministers are the mere servants of Christ; they have no authority of their own; their whole business is to do what they are commanded."[5] Paul is teaching that we serve completely under the direction of our Master.

Paul identifies one responsibility that lies at the heart of our stewardship: we're "stewards

---

4 John Calvin, *The Epistles of Paul the Apostle to the Corinthians*, Calvin's Commentaries, vol. XX (Grand Rapids: Baker, 2003), 150.

5 Charles Hodge, *1 & 2 Corinthians*, Geneva Series of Commentaries (Carlisle, PA: Banner of Truth, 1983), 64.

of the *mysteries of God*" (emphasis added). The word "mystery" refers to truth that wasn't known beforehand in the Old Testament and could never be known apart from God revealing it. In the New Testament, "mystery" can refer exclusively to the gospel. For example, in Paul's letter to the Romans he writes, "Now to Him who is able to establish you according to my gospel and the preaching of Jesus Christ, according to the revelation of the mystery which has been kept secret for long ages past…to the only wise God, through Jesus Christ, be the glory forever. Amen" (Rom. 16:25, 27). Thankfully, God chose to reveal this truth in the New Testament, and it no longer remains a mystery.

In 1 Corinthians 4:1, Paul uses the plural "mysteries" to include all the truths God has revealed. In other words, we're stewards of the totality of Scripture, including the glorious gospel of our Lord Jesus Christ.

As shepherds in Christ's church, we have many responsibilities in protecting and caring for the sheep (Titus 1:9). However, our chief duty is to *feed* the sheep (John 21:15–19). Our main task is to dispense our Master's food to His people: we're simply to take His Word and give it to His people on a weekly basis.

During my years at Grace Community Church, John MacArthur often reminded us of our chief duty as preachers using a familiar analogy. He said preachers aren't chefs—our job is not to create the meal. Instead, we're waiters, and our job is to get it to the table without messing it up!

If we want to preserve our spiritual stability despite the responses we receive throughout our ministries, we have to remember and embrace our position as Christ's servants. We're under His orders, and we're responsible to oversee what belongs to Him. Most importantly, we're stewards of His Word. When we remember that we're merely servants, it prevents us from entertaining an elevated view of ourselves and guards us from holding a low view of our duty to Christ.

REMEMBER
THE REAL STANDARD

A second crucial perspective we need to have about our leadership is to remember the real standard.

The world's governments understand the importance of having legal standards for certain things in society, for example the weights and measures used in commerce. In the United States, our constitution gives Congress the power to fix the standard of weights and measures. It wasn't until after our constitution was written that Congress actually established a standard of weights and measures. Imagine what it was like to have no uniform set of standards. Commerce would have been extremely difficult.

In recent years, with the globalization of manufacturing, the problem of differing standards has returned. This is an ever-present reality when I shop for shirts. I have several shirts that I bought many years ago—and they still fit! However, when I recently went to the store and tried on shirts that purported to be the same size, I found that the fit varied wildly from shirt to shirt. Some of the shirts were so tight that it looked like they had been painted on my body; others hung off my shoulders like I had lost twenty pounds (I almost bought a couple of those just for the encouragement). It seemed like every shirt manufacturer had created their own standard.

Unfortunately, the same problem exists in the church today. There are countless standards used to measure ministry success, but all of them are seriously flawed except for one. Paul asserts that there's only one real standard of success in ministry when he writes, "In this case, moreover, it is required of stewards that one be found *trustworthy*" (1 Cor. 4:2; emphasis added). The word "trustworthy" can also be translated *faithful* (ESV). This wonderful word contains two critical nuances. First, in our relationship to our Master, Jesus Christ, we're to be loyal to Him. Second, in our duties to Him, we're to be dependable.

Our Lord's standard of success, then, is for us to be loyal and dependable in carrying out the duties He has assigned. The New Testament praises several men for being faithful in their assignments: Timothy (1 Cor. 4:17), Tychicus (Eph. 6:21; Col. 4:7), Epaphras (Col. 1:7), Sylvanus (1 Pet. 5:12), and Moses (Heb. 3:5). Of course, the ultimate standard of faithfulness is our Lord Himself. The writer of Hebrews says, "He [Jesus] was faithful to Him [God] who appointed Him, as Moses also was in all His house" (Heb. 3:2). It's faithfulness that defines our Lord. In fact, when He returns at His Second Coming, the book of Revelation says that He "is called Faithful" (Rev. 19:11). The Gospel of John teaches that Jesus was faithful to His heavenly Father by only doing His will (John 5:19–20) and only speaking His words (John

12:49). Jesus was perfectly loyal to His Father in all things, and He was utterly dependable in the divine tasks that were assigned to Him (Mark 10:45; Luke 19:10).

It's both humbling and encouraging that our perfectly faithful Lord will evaluate our service based primarily on our faithfulness, not the results. New Testament theologian Gordon Fee writes, "Not eloquence nor wisdom (nor 'initiative,' nor 'success'—the more standard requirements), but faithfulness to the trust, is what God requires of his servants."[6] John Piper adds, "The Lord rewards faithfulness above fruitfulness, which puts us all on the same footing, whether famous for our effectiveness or unknown in our faithfulness."[7] The demand for faithfulness reminds us that our ultimate allegiance must first and foremost be to Christ. It must not be given to a Christian leader,

---

6 Gordon Fee, *The First Epistle to the Corinthians*, New International Commentary on the New Testament, rev. ed. (Grand Rapids: Eerdmans, 2014), 175.

7 John Piper, *A Godward Life: Seeing the Supremacy of God in All of Life* (Colorado Springs, CO: Waterbrook & Multnomah, 2015), 178.

denomination, theological tradition, academic institution, or even our own church. Rather, we must be faithful to our Lord and Master, Jesus Christ.

In the context of 1 Corinthians 4, Paul's primary emphasis is on faithfulness as stewards of God's mysteries. This high calling demands that we examine our own hearts and consider faithfulness in ministry: Do we faithfully proclaim God's Word and not our own? Do we earnestly seek to live in accordance with what we teach? Do we guard the treasure of sound doctrine from error (2 Tim. 1:12–14)? Do we refute those who contradict it (Titus 1:9)? Are we faithfully committing the true gospel to the next generation (2 Tim. 2:2)? We're called to be faithful stewards with the things God has entrusted to us.

There are many ways we can be *unfaithful* stewards of the mysteries of God:

1. Spending inadequate time to prepare to preach God's Word.

2. Treating the Word of God lightly by preaching messages that were prepared with little thought and effort, in some cases prepared in a couple of hours on a Saturday night.
3. Delivering sermons that were purchased or stolen from the internet.
4. Forcing a passage to say what it doesn't say because we want to make a specific point.
5. Downplaying the primacy and priority of the Word of God in our corporate worship services.
6. Creating messages that are more about what we want to say rather than explaining what God has already said.
7. Failing to apply the truth personally.
8. Exercising our gifts inconsistently rather than to their maximum potential, either due to laziness or distractions.

Being faithful doesn't mean showing up every week with something to say—everybody does that. Instead, being faithful means that, week after week, we do the hard, time-consuming work required to accurately handle the word of God (2 Tim. 2:15). Then, on the Lord's Day, we rightly explain the mysteries of God to His people. If those things are what motivate and drive you, regardless of the trials or triumphs of that week, be encouraged: you're biblically pursuing the real standard of ministry success.

REMEMBER THE REAL VERDICT

If we're going to develop a biblical perspective about our leadership, we must, thirdly, remember the real verdict.

Much of what undermines our stability in ministry is listening to premature judgments about our effectiveness from people whose opinions don't ultimately matter. This is true whether their assessment is positive or negative.

THE CHURCH'S ASSESSMENT DOESN'T MATTER

In 1 Corinthians 4:3–5, Paul reminds us that there are premature assessments of our lives and ministries that don't matter. Paul writes, "But to me it is a very small thing that I may be examined by you" (4:3). The word "examined" literally means to conduct a judicial hearing. In the New Testament, it's most often used of official legal proceedings. Some of the Corinthians saw themselves as the judge and jury of Paul's ministry. They claimed the right to personally sit in judgment on his leadership. In fact, in 1 Corinthians 9:3, Paul uses the same word to refer to those who are examining his character and putting his ministry on trial.

However, for Paul, the fact that some in the church of Corinth were putting him on trial was, by his own admission, an insignificant matter. Because some of the Corinthians either elevated him as their hero or snubbed him as their enemy, he responded by saying, in effect, it's trivial whether they lionize or demonize him.

Paul's attitude must be embraced by anyone in church ministry. We must never measure our success by whether we live up to, or fail to live up to, the expectations of other Christians, even those in our own church. The people in your church, and mine, aren't the ultimate judges of our ministry and service.

This doesn't mean that their criticism won't hurt, and it doesn't mean that you should never listen to your critics to see if there's a degree of truth in what they say. It's possible that your preaching *does* need to improve, or that you *are* making too many changes too quickly and you need to slow down. Perhaps your leadership skills are weak, or your style is too strong. Paul is not advocating that we reject godly counsel, especially that of older, mature men (Prov. 11:14; 15:22; 24:6). John Calvin rightly says,

> "It is part of a good pastor to submit both his doctrine and his life for examination to the judgment of the Church, and that it is the sign of a good conscience not to shun the light of careful inspection."[8]

Paul is not discrediting the advice of godly men. Rather, he's saying that their assessment of

---

8   Calvin, *The Epistles of Paul the Apostle to the Corinthians*, 152.

us is not the ultimate measure of our ministry success. Whether our churches highly honor or criticize us, they're not the final judge. We must be open to counsel and sensitive to criticism, but we must never forget that the Lord alone will judge our success.

There is, however, a danger we must guard against: even though we know the assessment of fellow Christians doesn't ultimately matter, we can still be tempted to change our philosophy of ministry to gain their approval. Whether it's pressure from our own members or from the Christian community in general, there's always the temptation to follow the hottest ministry trends and latest church fads—and there are many!

One current trend is to intentionally pursue having a "mega church." It's true that the church in Jerusalem was a large church (Acts 2:41; 4:4), but most New Testament churches were small (Acts 16:11–15; Rom. 16:3–5). Congregation size is not a biblical standard of success—it's not even an accurate one. The average church in the

United States has 186 attenders. However, that average is highly skewed by a number of mega churches. According to the National Congregation Study, the median church in the United States has seventy-five regular participants in worship on Sunday mornings. Churches with 350 or more attending on Sunday mornings are in the top ten percent of church attendance in the country. These statistics reveal that church size is certainly not the standard we should use to judge a ministry. In spite of that, we often feel pressure about the number of people in our churches.

There are many other ministry trends we could be pressured to follow:

1. The latest style of music and musical instruments.
2. Trendy facilities that bear no resemblance to a traditional church.
3. Emphasizing the culture's view of justice (social justice).
4. Trying to connect with the culture by

having tattoos and piercings and wearing trendy clothes.
5. Using video clips in our sermons.
6. Sharing relevant, relational messages.
7. Having multiple campuses and church sites.
8. Holding multiple services to accommodate various styles of music.

If we aren't careful, we can allow the judgment of other Christians, including our own members, to define what constitutes a successful ministry. When that happens, unlike with Paul, it's not a small thing to be examined by others. Rather, it has become a big thing—it matters way too much! Just like Paul, we must remember that the church's assessment of us is not of primary importance.

THE WORLD'S ASSESSMENT DOESN'T MATTER

A second assessment that doesn't really matter is that of the world. Paul writes, "But to me it is a very small thing that I may be examined by you *or by any human court*" (4:3; emphasis added). The expression "by any human court" can literally be translated "by man's day." It's very much like our expression "having one's day in court." Here, Paul is speaking of people in a general sense. Because this statement is contrasted with those in the church (4:3a), he's primarily referring to those outside the church, those who are in the world.

Ministry success cannot be measured by how much we live up to the expectations of the court of fallen human opinion, from those who cannot "accept the things of the Spirit of God" (1 Cor. 2:14). They have unredeemed hearts and minds (Rom. 1:18–24; 2 Cor. 4:4; Eph. 2:2–3) and are in a current state of perishing (1 Cor. 1:18; 2 Cor. 4:3). The unbelievers in Corinth, both Jews and Greeks, had evaluated Paul's life and ministry and concluded that his message was foolish and moronic. 1 Corinthians 1:18–25 describes their conclusion:

The word of the cross is foolishness to those who are perishing, but to us who are being saved it is the power of God. For it is written, "I WILL DESTROY THE WISDOM OF THE WISE, AND THE CLEVERNESS OF THE CLEVER I WILL SET ASIDE." Where is the wise man? Where is the scribe? Where is the debater of this age? Has not God made foolish the wisdom of the world? For since in the wisdom of God the world through its wisdom did not *come to* know God, God was well-pleased through the foolishness of the message preached to save those who believe. For indeed Jews ask for signs and Greeks search for wisdom; but we preach Christ crucified, to Jews a stumbling block and to Gentiles foolishness, but to those who are the called, both Jews and Greeks, Christ the power of God and the wisdom of God. Because the foolishness of God is wiser than men, and the weakness of God is stronger than men.

According to Paul, the good news of the cross of Christ was utter foolishness to the unbelieving world around him. The Gentiles rejected the message because they believed it to be foolishness (v. 22). The Jews rejected Paul's message because a crucified, dead Messiah made no sense to them—it was a stumbling block (v. 23). The Greek word for "stumbling block" is the basis for our English word *scandal*. The idea of a crucified Messiah was offensive and scandalous to the Jewish community.

Nevertheless, Paul refused to let the world's verdict alter his message and ministry methods. Despite the immense pressure in Corinth, Paul never caved on the gospel. In fact, he proclaimed, "I determined to know nothing among you except Jesus Christ and him crucified" (1 Cor. 2:2). Even though his enemies and detractors said his message was foolish, Paul doubled down on His previous gospel claim (1:18).

The world will always place enormous pressure on the church and its leaders to change its theology, doctrine, and practice to gain their favorable assessment. Those who desire the world's favor and the culture's acceptance must be prepared to compromise in areas like these:

1. Be inclusive instead of exclusive when it comes to the truth of the gospel (Matt. 7:13–14), to acknowledge that there are many ways to heaven, not just one (John 14:7).
2. Reject a grammatical-historical approach to interpreting the Bible.
3. Accept macro-evolution as the only reasonable explanation for the origins of the earth, rejecting a literal six-day creation.
4. Agree that homosexuality and same-sex marriage aren't sinful.
5. Embrace gender fluidity, teaching that gender is not fixed at conception but rather is fluid based on personal preferences.

Pastors who affirm those tenets and similar ones will, without a doubt, earn the world's favor and its positive assessment of their ministry.

Sadly, individual Christians, whole churches, entire denominations, and many Christian colleges and seminaries have capitulated to the world's pressures and demands. Biblical truth has been exchanged for pragmatic, seeker-friendly ideas in hopes of receiving a favorable verdict from the world. We must recognize that what the world thinks of us doesn't matter.

OUR PERSONAL ASSESSMENT DOESN'T MATTER

A third assessment that doesn't really matter is our own assessment. Paul writes, "...in fact, I do not even examine myself. For I am conscious of nothing against myself" (4:3–4). The Greek verb translated "I am conscious" is the root from which the noun *conscience* comes. The conscience is a courtroom within our souls where our moral decisions are constantly on trial. The role of conscience is to evaluate us against God's Law, the substance of which is written on every man's heart (Rom. 2:14–15).

Paul argues that his conscience defended his character and conduct in ministry. The deliberate word ordering of the Greek stresses the word "nothing" to highlight the fact that his conscience is *completely* clear. What exactly does Paul mean by this? First, in a general sense, Paul's conscience was clear from any unrepentant, unconfessed sin. He makes that point in 2 Corinthians 1:12 when he says, "Our proud confidence is this: the testimony of our conscience, that in holiness and godly sincerity, not in fleshly wisdom but in the grace of God, we have conducted ourselves in the world, and especially toward you." Paul may have meant that in the overarching, general sense of sin, his conscience was clear. Certainly, that was true.

Second, and more likely, the context suggests that Paul meant he wasn't aware of any significant failure in his stewardship and service. 1 Corinthians 4:4 seems to indicate this: "For I am conscious of nothing against myself, yet I am not by this acquitted." In the New Testament, the Greek word for "acquitted" is normally translated "justify"

(Rom. 3:20, 24, 26). Paul says he's not justified by the fact that he doesn't know of any failures in his ministry. Having a clear conscience toward one's conduct in ministry doesn't mean that Jesus Christ agrees. The book of Proverbs makes this very point: "Every man's way is right in his own eyes, but the Lord weighs the hearts" (Prov. 22:1). If a policeman pulls you over for speeding, try telling him, "You can't give me a ticket, my conscience is clear!"

Paul's point is not that we should avoid self-examination, but rather that our personal assessment of our ministry is inadequate. Whether we're satisfied with the state of our ministry or feel completely ineffective and unsuccessful, assessing our own ministry is as inadequate as an employee conducting his own performance evaluation. 2 Corinthians 10:18 says, "It is not he who commends himself that is approved, but he whom the Lord commends." That's why Paul doesn't judge his own ministry. Your assessment of the effectiveness and faithfulness of your ministry is ultimately insignificant.

In reality, there's only one verdict that truly matters: the Lord's. Paul says, "But the one who examines me is the Lord" (4:4). Gordon Fee writes, "Only the Lord, the master of the house, to whom alone I am accountable, may examine me and hand down a verdict as to the faithfulness with which I discharge my duties."[9] According to Revelation 1, Jesus is walking in the midst of the seven churches ("lampstands"), evaluating, reviewing, and inspecting their conduct. Then, He sends His perfect evaluation to each of them (Rev. 2–3). What a sobering reality! He continues to do the same today.

A day is coming when Christ will tell each of us—face to face—His honest assessment of our ministry. Paul writes, "Therefore, do not go on passing judgment before the time, but wait until the Lord comes" (4:5). Paul lived under the constant awareness of the coming judgment and evaluation of his life and ministry. He understood there was no escaping this reality. In 2 Corinthians

---

9   Fee, *The First Epistle to the Corinthians*, 177.

5:10 he writes, "We must all appear before the judgment seat of Christ, so that each one may be recompensed for his deeds in the body, according to what he has done, whether good or bad."

The only assessment that truly matters is that which comes from Christ. All other judgments and assessments are premature. We ought to patiently wait until Christ returns, and He will reveal the true verdict on our ministries.

This doesn't mean that we shouldn't speak out against error or confront sin and compromise. Paul makes that clear when he says, "What have I to do with judging outsiders? Do you not judge those who are within the church?" (1 Cor. 5:12). He commands the Corinthians to judge those inside the church through church discipline (see Matt. 18:15–20). Later, he tells them to mediate disputes among the brothers: "I say this to your shame. Is it so, that there is not among you one wise man who will be able to decide between his brethren…?" (1 Cor. 6:5). Paul spoke out publicly against those whose lives or teaching were contrary to Scripture. Simon Kistemaker writes,

> "[Paul] is not saying that they should suspend judging altogether. Surely not! When a pastor or teacher fails to adhere to the truth of God's word and in his teaching and life goes contrary to the Scriptures, the church must judge. But Paul forbids criticizing a person whose teaching and conduct are in harmony with Scripture."[10]

Paul doesn't say we should suspend all judgment inside the church; rather, he highlights that the Lord's final verdict is the only one that matters because only He knows the entire story. Only He knows the motives of the heart (John 2:24; Rev. 1:14)! Most importantly, only the Master has the right to judge His servants. Romans 14:4 says, "Who are you to judge the servant of another?

---

10 Simon J. Kistemaker, *1 Corinthians*, New Testament Commentary (Grand Rapids: Baker, 1993), 132.

To his own master he stands or falls." Christ will certainly—without exception—evaluate and judge our service.

First Corinthians 3:12–15 describes Christ's future judgment:

> Now if any man builds on the foundation with gold, silver, precious stones, wood, hay, straw, each man's work will become evident; for the day will show it because it is *to be* revealed with fire, and the fire itself will test the quality of each man's work. If any man's work which he has built on it remains, he will receive a reward. If any man's work is burned up, he will suffer loss; but he himself will be saved, yet so as through fire.

This passage features Christ's penetrating omniscience that will be used in His judgment of our ministries and service, and ultimately our hearts. Paul describes this judgment as a fire sweeping through the building we're supposed to be constructing. If it's built with the right materials it will survive, but if it's built with the wrong materials, it will be destroyed. The measure of a successful ministry, then, is building with the right materials: gold, silver, and precious stones (v. 12).

ONLY CHRIST'S ASSESSMENT MATTERS

Paul returns to the theme of future judgment and gives two criteria that Christ will use to evaluate his servants: faithfulness and motives. These are the right materials we must use in constructing the building.

Christ's Assessment of Our Faithfulness

Concerning faithfulness, Paul writes, "Therefore do not go on passing judgment before the time, but wait until the Lord comes who will…bring to light the things hidden in the darkness…" (4:5). The phrase "things hidden" often speaks of things that are evil. For example, 2 Corinthians 4:2 refers to "the things hidden because of shame." A man's character and ministry may look perfect on the outside, rendering a positive verdict; however, there may be "hidden things" that, if known, would produce an entirely different verdict. D. A. Carson writes, "There are some leaders who function competently and can please great crowds, but whose hearts are seething swamps of lust, arrogance, and ambition."[11] God will bring to light the things hidden in the darkness.

But in 1 Corinthians 4:5, Paul is not only referring to hidden sin, but also to acts of service and ministry that are hidden to others, quite possibly even to ourselves. At the Second Coming of Christ, in a specific judgment known as the Judgment of Nations, true disciples will stand before Christ and He will say to them:

> For I was hungry, and you gave Me *something* to eat; I was thirsty, and you gave Me *something* to drink; I was a stranger, and you invited Me in; naked, and you clothed Me; I was sick,

---

11 D. A. Carson, *The Cross & Christian Ministry: Leadership Lessons from 1 Corinthians* (Grand Rapids: Baker, 2005), 100-01.

and you visited Me; I was in prison, and you came to Me.' Then the righteous will answer Him, 'Lord, when did we see You hungry, and feed You, or thirsty, and give You *something* to drink? And when did we see You a stranger, and invite You in, or naked, and clothe You? When did we see You sick, or in prison, and come to You?' [Matt. 25:35–40]

Jesus is saying if you did good deeds to the least of my brethren, you ultimately did it to Me. At the future judgment, Christ will bring to light the hidden acts of service we didn't even realize that God, in His grace, had accomplished through us. What an amazing reality!

Christ's Assessment of Our Motives

The second criterion Christ will use to evaluate his servants is our motives. Paul says that the Lord will "disclose the motives of *men's* hearts" (4:5). Motives are an essential part of what determines our eternal reward. It's not enough to teach the truth of God's Word faithfully and accurately; we must also be willing to do so for the glory of the Master rather than our own. John Calvin writes,

> "This passage…militates, not merely against wicked teachers, but also against all that have any other object in view than the glory of Christ and the edification of the Church. For every one that teaches the truth is not necessarily faithful, but only he who desires from the heart to serve the Lord and advance Christ's kingdom."[12]

We're to serve God for His glory and His name's sake, which means we're to serve out of love for Christ and His people (1 John 2:9–11). These are the motives that must compel us.

In the first three chapters of 1 Corinthians, Paul develops a recurring contrast—the contrast between his motives and the motives of some of the leaders in Corinth. In these contrasts, Paul

---

12 Calvin, *The Epistles of Paul the Apostle to the Corinthians*, 151.

identifies both right and wrong motives that can govern our ministries.

First, we must be motivated by a desire to encourage loyalty to Christ rather than loyalty to ourselves. First Corinthians 1:10–17 teaches that it's vital for your people to be loyal to Christ rather than to your own group or movement.

Second, we must be motivated by a desire to elevate the glory of God rather than our own glory (1:18–31). Do you want people to think of you as intelligent, cultured, and educated? Or are you content to be thought of as foolish, weak, despised, base, and absolutely nothing? Are you in ministry for your glory, or God's glory?

Third, we must be motivated by a desire to promote the wisdom of God revealed in the Word of God, as opposed to our own wisdom and cleverness (2:1–16). Do you desire that your people think you're cool, edgy, and clever, or are you more concerned that their faith rests on the power of God? Do you want the people who sit under your preaching to be more impressed with you and your wisdom, or with the wisdom of Christ? Do you want them to understand your mind, or the mind of Christ?

Fourth, we must be motivated by a desire to magnify the work of God rather than our own accomplishments (3:1–9). Do you think of yourself as a slave of Christ? Do you constantly remind yourself and others that your gifts are from God, through Christ, and that any results are a product of the work of God? We must be on guard against elevating our own accomplishments, because Christ will not only examine our faithfulness, but also our motives.

OUR HEAVENLY REWARD

Paul continues to describe Christ's assessment: "…and then each man's praise will come to him from God" (4:5). This could literally be translated "then the praise will come to each one from God." Through Christ our Judge, our Father will express His approval and praise of the faithful servant. This is reminiscent of the master's response in the Parable of the Talents: "'Well done good and faithful slave. You were faithful with a few things,

I will put you in charge of many things; enter into the joy of your master'" (Matt. 25:21). Jesus' parable reminds us that our reward will consist primarily of two components: a greater capacity for service in eternity and, remarkably, praise from our Lord! Both Jesus and Paul acknowledge the rewards that come to a faithful steward.

After learning that the Lord will examine our faithfulness, shine light on hidden things, and disclose the motives of all hearts, a reward is the last thing we would expect! However, His reward shouldn't surprise us, because that's just like our God: He's incredibly generous and gracious in every way. And on that Day, He will reward our service to Him. Matthew Henry writes,

> "Though none of God's servants can deserve anything from him, though there be much that is blamable even in their best services, yet shall their fidelity be commended and crowned by him."[13]

---

13 Matthew Henry, *A Commentary on the Whole Bible*, vol. VI (Old Tappan, NJ: Fleming H. Revell), 523.

Unfortunately, there will be some church leaders who receive no praise because they used worthless materials to build, and their work will be burned up (1 Cor. 3:15). However, like the seven churches in the book of Revelation, most will receive commendation from our Lord (Rev. 2–3). Even with their struggles, five of the churches received His commendation. Likewise, our Lord will shower His praise on the one who is faithful today. What an amazing truth!

I often find myself asking, "How can I receive praise from the Lord when my service is imperfect and my motives are always mixed?" The answer is the gospel. The Westminster Confession of Faith says,

"The persons of believers being accepted through Christ, their good works also are accepted in Him, not as though they were in this life wholly unblameable and unreprovable in God's sight; but that He, looking up them in His son, is pleased to accept and reward that which is sincere, although accompanied with many weaknesses and imperfections."[14]

D. A. Carson adds,

"How wonderful! The King of the universe, the Sovereign who has endured our endless rebellion and sought us out at the cost of His Son's death, climaxes our redemption by praising us!"[15]

What amazing grace from our King!

What does all this mean for you? You might be serving in a difficult place where you feel you're in the trenches. You might be discouraged and distraught and at times feel all alone. Maybe you serve in a church where there's mutual care and respect among the leadership and members, where the word of God is thriving

---

14 *Westminster Confession of Faith* (Glasgow, Scotland: Free Presbyterian Publications, 1995), 71.
15 Carson, *The Cross and Christian Ministry*, 101.

and people are growing. Or perhaps you serve in a church very much like Corinth, where both positive and negative perspectives of you and your ministry exist simultaneously. Whatever your circumstance, if you want to survive the trials and triumphs of church ministry, you must do what the apostle Paul did: remember your real position. You're a steward of Christ. And faithfulness is the real standard.

You must also remember the real verdict. It's not the church's assessment, or the world's, or even your own that really matters. You have one Master, and only His evaluation matters. As fellow stewards in the household of God, we must strive to live our lives and conduct our ministries in light of this truth. And if we do, at Christ's Second Coming, our praise will come directly to us from God our Father!

"STEWARDS"
A SERMON BY CHARLES SPURGEON[1]

"Let a man so account of us, as of the ministers of Christ, and stewards of the mysteries of God. Moreover, it is required in stewards that a man be found faithful."

1 Cor. 4:1–2

The Office of a Faithful Steward

1. A steward is a servant and no more.
2. A steward is a servant under the more immediate command of the great Master.
3. A steward is constantly giving an account.
4. A steward is a trustee of his Master's goods.

---

[1] This sermon was preached by Charles Haddon Spurgeon in 1887 at the Annual Conference of the Pastors' College Association. The outline points and quote are taken and adapted from that sermon. *From The Metropolitan Tabernacle Pulpit*, 63 vols, (Pasadena, TX: Pilgrim, 1913), sermon #3350. www.spurgeongems.org

5. A steward's business is to dispense his Master's goods according to their design.

6. A steward is the guardian of his Master's family.

7. A steward represents his Master.

How to Be an Unfaithful Steward

1. Acting as a chief instead of servant.

2. Acting as a men-pleaser.

3. Being an idler and trifler.

4. Misusing the Master's property.

5. Neglecting any one of the family or any portion of the estate.

6. Conniving at evil.

7. Forgetting that the Master is coming.

My heart and my flesh tremble while I contemplate the possibility of anyone of us being found guilty of treachery to our charge and treason to our King. May the good Lord so abide with us, that at the last we may be clear of the blood of all men. It will be seven heavens in one to hear our Master say, 'Well done, good and faithful servant.'

VOICES FROM THE PAST

ORIGEN (CA. 185-253)

There is a big difference between being a servant of Christ and a steward of the mysteries of God. Anyone who has read the Bible can be a servant of Christ, but to be a steward of the mysteries one must plumb their depths.[1]

JOHN CHRYSOSTOM (CA. 347-407)

A steward's duty is to administer well the things that have been entrusted to him. The things of the master's are not the stewards but the reverse—what is his really belongs to the master.[2]

---

1 Origen, *Commentary on 1 Corinthians*, 2.18.10-6, JTS 9:354.
2 John Chrysostom, *Homilies on the Epistles of Paul to the Corinthians*, 10.5, NPNF 1 12:56.

THEODORET OF CYR (CA. 393-457)

No banker plays fast and loose with other people's deposits. Rather he looks after them in order to keep them safe for the one who has entrusted them to him.[3]

JOHN CALVIN (1509-1564)

For it is not the case that everyone who teaches the truth is consistently faithful, but only the person who desires from the bottom of his heart to serve the Lord and to advance the Kingdom of Christ.[4]

---

3 Theodoret of Cyr, *Commentary on the First Epistle to the Corinthians*, 188, Migne PG 82:255.
4 John Calvin, *Calvin's New Testament Commentaries*, vol. 9, *The First Epistle of Paul to the Corinthians* (Grand Rapids: Eerdmans, 1979), 85.

RICHARD BAXTER (1615-1691)

The ministerial work must be carried on purely for God and the salvation of souls, not for any private ends of our own.... They who engage in this as a common work, to make a trade of it for their worldly livelihood, will find that they have chosen a bad trade, though a good employment. Self-denial is of absolute necessity in every Christian, but it is doubly necessary in a minister, as without it he cannot do God an hour's faithful service.[5]

MATTHEW HENRY (1662-1714)

The ministers of Christ should make it their hearty and continual endeavor to approve themselves trustworthy; and when they have the testimony of a good conscience, and the approbation of their master, they must slight the opinions and censures of their fellow-servants.[6]

---

5 Richard Baxter, *The Reformed Pastor* (Carlisle, PA: Banner of Truth, 2007), 111.

6 Matthew Henry, *Matthew Henry's Commentary on the Whole Bible, vol. 6, Acts to Revelation* (Peabody, MA: Hendrickson, 1991), 421.

CHARLES BRIDGES (1794-1869)

If the family of Christ be a household, the Minister is 'the faithful and wise steward,' who dispenses the provision of the house according to the necessities of its several members.[7]

CHARLES HODGE (1797-1878)

The great thing required of [ministers] is fidelity. Fidelity to Christ as servants; not arrogating to themselves any other than ministerial power, or venturing to go beyond his commands. Fidelity also to the people, not failing to dispense to them the truths which God has revealed, nor mixing those truths with their own speculations, much less substituting for those doctrines human knowledge or wisdom.[8]

---

7 Charles Bridges, *The Christian Ministry* (Carlisle, PA: Banner of Truth, 2022), 12.

8 Charles Hodge, *Commentary on the First Epistle to the Corinthians* (Grand Rapids: Eerdmans, 1974), 65.

CHARLES SPURGEON (1832-1892)

If we magnify ourselves, we shall become contemptible; and we shall neither magnify our office nor our Lord. We are the servants of Christ, and not lords over His heritage.[9]

R. C. H. LENSKI (1864-1936)

"Trustworthy" means: so that his master may completely rely on him. The word is to be viewed wholly from the master's standpoint: "trustworthy" in the judgment and according to the verdict of the master. Our heavenly Master makes no mistake in judging the trustworthiness of the ministers to whom he has entrusted the gospel and the church.[10]

---

9 Charles H. Spurgeon, *An All-round Ministry* (Carlisle, PA: Banner of Truth, 1978), 256.
10 R. C. H. Lenski, *The Interpretation of St. Paul's First and Second Epistles to the Corinthians* (Minneapolis, MN: Augsburg, 1963), 164.

J. GRESHAM MACHEN (1881-1937)

God make us, whatever else we are, just faithful messengers, who present, without fear or favour, not our word, but the Word of God![11]

JOHN R. W. STOTT (1921-2011)

The preacher is a steward of God's mysteries, that is, of the self-revelation which God has entrusted to men and which is now preserved in the Scriptures. The Christian preacher's message, therefore, is derived not directly from the mouth of God, as if he were a prophet or apostle, nor from his own mind, like the false prophets, nor undigested from the minds and mouths of other men, like the babbler, but from the once revealed and now recorded Word of God, of which he is a privileged steward.[12]

---

11 J. Gresham Machen, *God Transcendent* (Carlisle, PA: Banner of Truth, 1982), 133.
12 John R. W. Stott, *The Preacher's Portrait* (Grand Rapids: Eerdmans, 1977), 17.

JOHN MACARTHUR (1939-)

God supplies His Word, His Spirit, His gifts, and His power. All that the minister can supply is his faithfulness in using those resources. The work is demanding but is basically simple: taking God's Word and feeding it faithfully to His people—dispensing the mysteries of God, proclaiming the hidden truths He has made known. There is to be no glory here, ranking one above the other. The best that any minister can be is faithful, which is just fulfilling the basic requirement.[13]

---

13 John MacArthur, *1 Corinthians, MacArthur New Testament Commentary* (Chicago, IL: Moody, 1984), 100.

SCRIPTURE INDEX

EXODUS

19–31 13

1 KINGS

18–19 13

PROVERBS

11:14 39
15:22 39
22:1 49
24:6 39

MATTHEW

7:13–14 46
25:21 59
25:35–40 56

MARK

3:20–27 13
10:43–44 24
10:45 32

LUKE

12:42 25
16:1 25
16:3 25
19:10 32

JOHN

2:24	52
5:19–20	31
12:49	32
14:7	46
17:17	7
21:15–17	8, 28

ACTS

2:41	40
4:4	40
16:11–15	40

ROMANS

2:14–15	47
3:20–26	48
14:4	52
16:3–5	27
16:25	27
16:27	27

1 CORINTHIANS

1:10–17	58
1:11–12	18
1:18,	43, 45
1:18–25	43
1:18–31	58
2:1–5	15
2:1–16	58
2:2	45
2:14	43
3:1–9	59
3:4	15
3:5	21, 22
3:9	22
3:12–15	53
3:15	61
4:17	31
5:12	51
6:5	51
9:1–18	15
9:3	38

2 CORINTHIANS

1:12	48
3:18	7
4:2	54
4:3	43
4:4	43
5:10	50
10:18	49

GALATIANS

4:1–2	25

EPHESIANS

2:2–3	43
5:18	23
6:21	31

COLOSSIANS

1:7	31
1:18	23
4:7	31

2 TIMOTHY

1:12–14	33
2:2	33
2:15	8, 35

TITUS

1:7	25
1:9	28, 33

HEBREWS

3:2	31
3:5	31

JAMES

1:18	7

1 PETER

5:12	31

1 JOHN

2:9–11	57

REVELATION

1–3	50, 61
1:14	52
19:11	31

ABOUT THE AUTHOR

Tom Pennington has served as Pastor-Teacher at Countryside Bible Church in Southlake, Texas since 2003. Prior to arriving in Texas, Tom served in various roles at Grace Community Church in Sun Valley, California for 16 years. His ministry at Grace included being an elder, Senior Associate Pastor, and the personal assistant to John MacArthur. Tom was also an adjunct faculty member of The Master's Seminary and Managing Director of Grace to You.

Tom is a graduate of Bob Jones University and holds an honorary Doctor of Divinity (D.D.) from The Master's University.

In addition to his role at Countryside, Tom travels internationally to train pastors in expository preaching.

He serves as Dean of the Dallas Distance Location at The Master's Seminary, teaches various seminary courses, and is actively involved internationally in training pastors in expository preaching.

Tom's preaching and teaching ministry at Countryside provides the source material for the content on The Word Unleashed.

FAITHFUL STEWARDS SERIES

· *Faithful Stewards* ·
· *A Biblical Case for Elder Rule* ·
· *All the World's a Stage* ·
· *Up From the Grave* ·
· *Preaching in the Spirit's Power* ·
· *Hallowed Be Your Name* ·
· *Blind Spot* ·

www.TheWordUnleashed.org

PERSONAL NOTES